Collins

easy learning

Writing
bumper book

Ages
3–5

apple

_anana

_ear

_range

Carol Medcalf

How to use this book

- Find a quiet, comfortable place to work, away from distractions.

- This book has been written in a logical order, so start at the first page and work your way through.

- Encourage your child to develop the correct grip by showing them how you hold a pencil. The use of the right or left hand is fine at this stage; it is normal for young children to use both hands before showing a preference.

- Help with reading the instructions where necessary and ensure that your child understands what to do.

- All children learn and develop at their own rate. If an activity is too difficult for your child then do more of our suggested practical activities (see Parent's tips) and return to the page when you know that they are likely to achieve it.

- Some children find it easier if all the other activities on the page are covered with a blank piece of paper, so only the activity they are working on is visible.

- Always end each activity before your child gets tired so that they will be eager to return next time.

- Help and encourage your child to check their own answers as they complete each activity.

- Let your child return to their favourite pages once they have been completed. Talk about the activities they enjoyed and what they have learned.

Special features of this book:

- **Parent's tip:** situated on every left-hand page, this suggests further activities and encourages discussion about what your child has learned.

- **Tracing activities:** talk about the shapes of the patterns and letters, and the pencil movement as your child writes, e.g. 'straight down with a little flick' for the letter 'l'.

- **Progress panel:** situated at the bottom of every right-hand page, the number of stars shows your child how far they have progressed through the book. Once they have completed each double page, ask them to colour in the blank star.

- **Certificate:** the certificate on the last page should be used to reward your child for their effort and achievement. Remember to give your child plenty of praise and encouragement, regardless of how they do.

Published by Collins
An imprint of HarperCollinsPublishers Ltd
The News Building
1 London Bridge Street
London
SE1 9GF

Browse the complete Collins catalogue at www.collins.co.uk

© HarperCollinsPublishers Ltd 2018

10 9 8 7 6

ISBN 9780008275419

The author asserts the moral right to be identified as the author of this work.

All rights reserved. No part of this publication may be reproduced, stored in a retrieval system, or transmitted, in any form or by any means, electronic, mechanical, photocopying, recording or otherwise, without the prior permission of Collins.

British Library Cataloguing in Publication Data

A Catalogue record for this publication is available from the British Library

All images and illustrations are © shutterstock.com and © HarperCollinsPublishers

Author: Carol Medcalf
Commissioning Editor: Michelle I'Anson
Project Manager: Rebecca Skinner
Cover Design: Sarah Duxbury
Text Design and Layout: Q2A Media
Illustration: Jenny Tulip
Production: Natalia Rebow
Printed in Great Britain by Bell and Bain Ltd.

Contents

Straight patterns

● Start at the red dot.
Trace the lines to finish the race.

To be able to write, it is important to develop a good pincer grip (using the thumb and index finger). To strengthen the relevant muscles, activities that encourage the same action will really help, such as working with playdough, threading beads or playing with Lego™.

4

Wavy patterns

● Start at the red dot.
  Trace the bumpy lines to help the cars on their way.

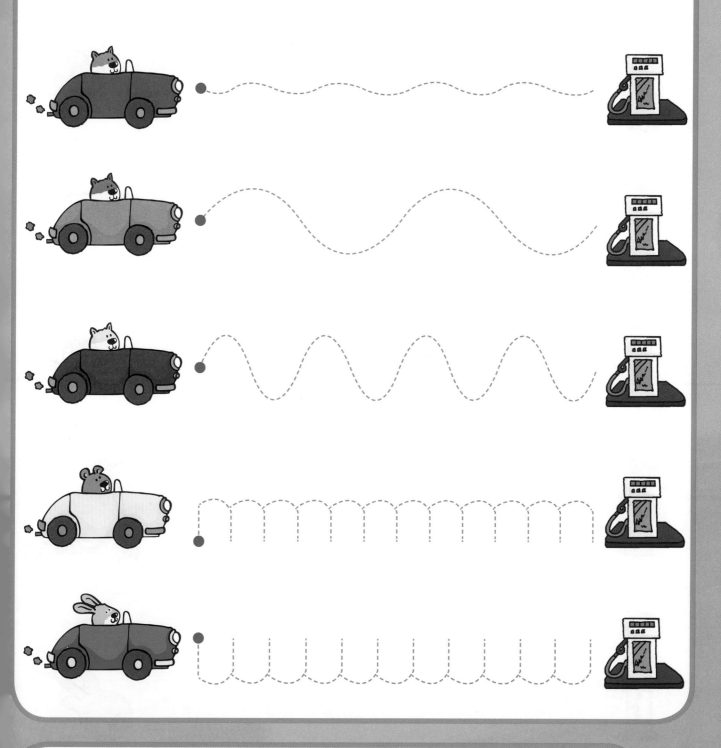

Well done!
Now colour
the star.

Curly patterns

● Start at the red dot.
Trace the curly lines to find each child's toy.

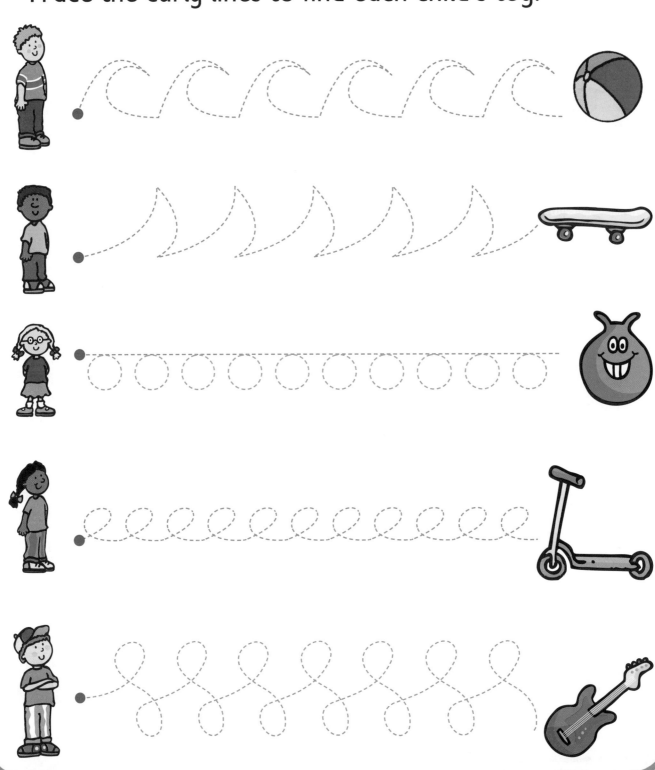

Further ideas for activities to develop the pincer grip include pouring rice or small beads from a small jug into a cup. If any grains of rice or beads are spilt, use the pincer grip to pick them up. To further this activity, use tweezers to pick up the rice or beads.

Colour match

- Match the brushes to the paint pots.
  Use the correct colour pen and stay in the middle of the two lines.

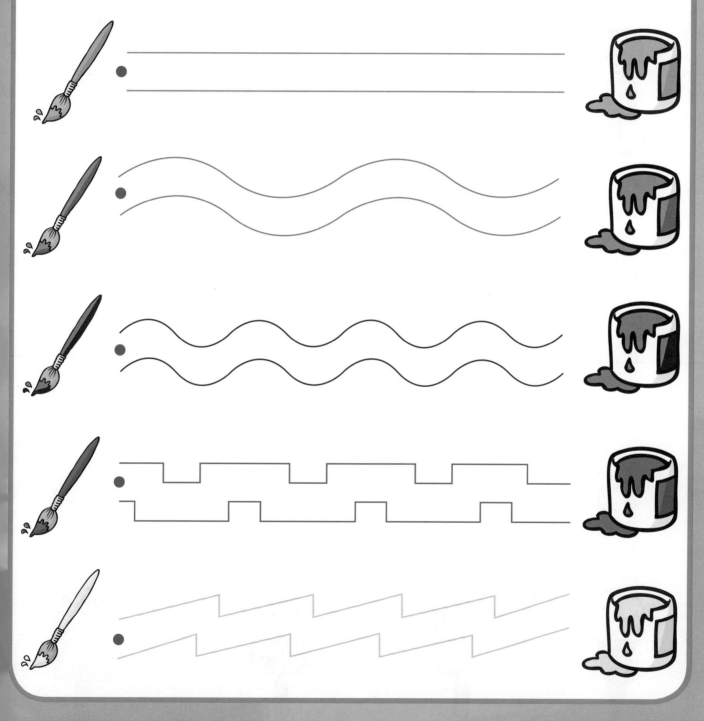

Well done!
Now colour
the star.

Ice cream race

The race is on! Who will get to their ice cream first? Draw between the lines.

Activities that make your child move their wrist are also helpful when learning to write. Mixing with a spoon while enjoying cooking is a great exercise, and a pestle and mortar can be used to grind herbs or even just leaves to make a mud pie in the garden.

Colouring fun

● Colour the pictures of the ice creams and lollies.

Well done!
Now colour
the star.

Drawing

- Copy the pictures.

- Draw your family in this picture frame.

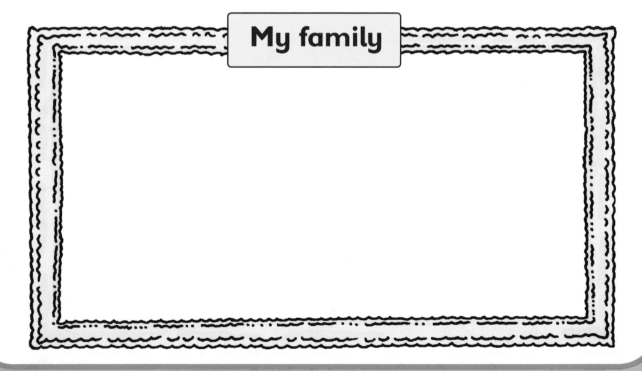

My family

Children often enjoy making still-life pictures. A few pieces of fruit, a flower or a favourite teddy are good objects to start with. Give them the correct colours and see what they produce. Drawing and colouring are perfect pre-writing skills.

Matching

● Draw lines to match the objects that go together.

Well done! Now colour the star. ☆☆☆☆

Dot-to-dot

● Join the dots in order from 1 to 10.

.	.	.	.	.	.	.	.	.	.
1	2	3	4	5	6	7	8	9	10

● Start at number 1. Join the dots to draw the picture. Then colour it in.

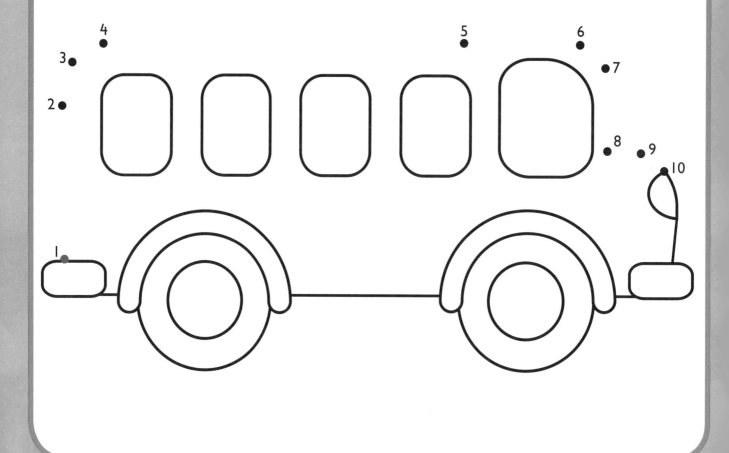

Writing with a finger in a thin layer of flour sprinkled on a tray provides lots of fun and is great writing practice. A progression from using a finger is a pen (with the lid on!) or a thin paintbrush – encourage the pincer grip to hold the pen or brush. Any form of mark making is valuable. The Easy Learning abc or Numbers Flashcards can be used here too, so your child has an example to copy.

Butterflies

● Copy the patterns to complete the butterflies.

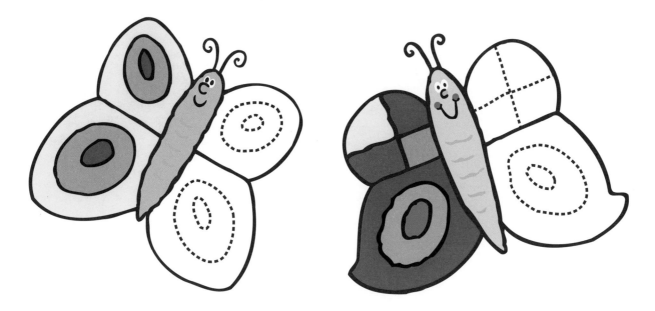

● Draw a line to match each caterpillar to a butterfly.

Well done!
Now colour
the star.

13

Shapes

● Join the dots to draw the shapes.

Draw large shapes in the air with your finger. Discuss the shape as you do so, e.g. a circle: 'draw round and back to the top' or a square: 'draw along, down, across the bottom and back up to the top'. Draw different shapes on each other's backs and try to guess what the shape is.

Shape pictures

● Copy the pictures made from shapes.

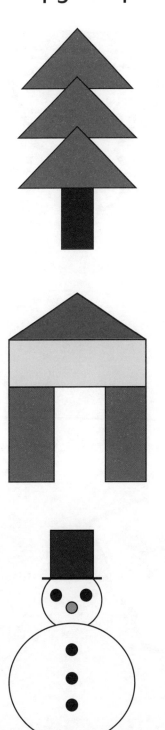

Around the world

● Start at the aeroplane and fly around the world.

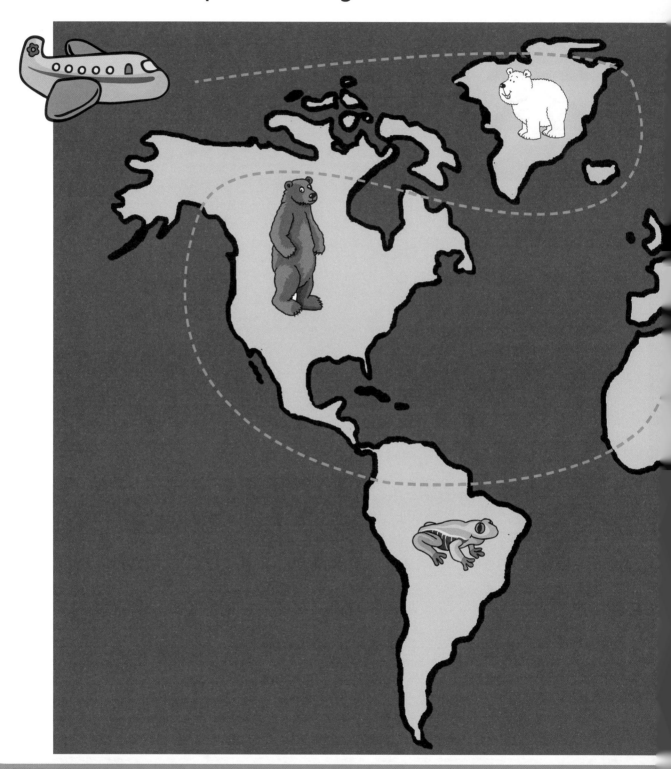

On a piece of paper, draw dashes or a faint line, making lots of different patterns and shapes, for your child to trace. This will encourage pen control and develop the movements needed for writing.

● Can you circle where you live?

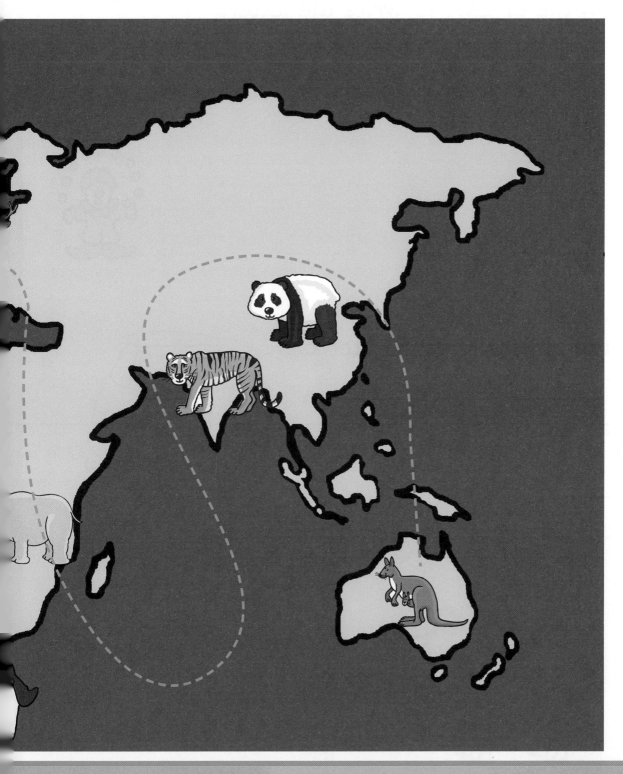

Well done!
Now colour
the star.
☆☆☆☆☆☆☆

Lowercase letter c

- **Start at the red dot.**
  Follow the arrows to write the letter.

- **Colour these pictures.**
  They all start with the letter c.

When learning to write letters, encourage your child to form the letters in one movement without taking the pen off the paper. For example, the letter 'a' should be written by going anti-clockwise round, back up to the top and down to the bottom again, rather than drawing a circle and then adding a line.

Lowercase letters o and a

- Start at the red dot.
  Follow the arrows to write the letter.

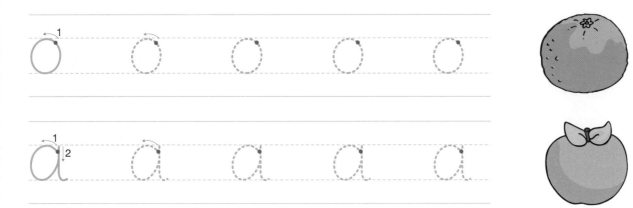

- Draw a line to match each picture to the correct letter.

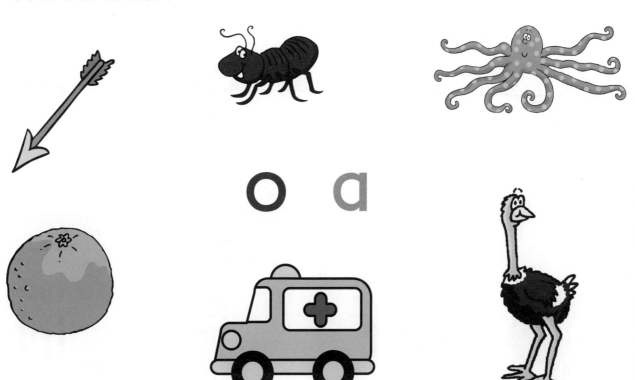

o a

Lowercase letters d and g

● Start at the red dot.
  Follow the arrows to write the letter.

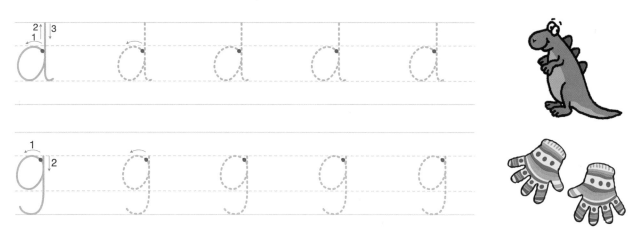

● Write **d** or **g** to complete each word.

duck

_og

goat

_irl

Cutting with scissors is a good skill to develop. Old greetings cards are excellent for cutting practice as they do not bend, making them easier to cut than paper. Make sure your child understands that they should only use scissors when supervised by you.

Lowercase letters i and r

- Start at the red dot.
  Follow the arrows to write the letter.

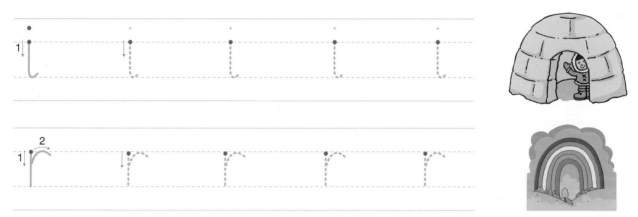

- With your pen, follow the footprints that the rabbit made after stepping in the ink.

Well done!
Now colour
the star.

21

Lowercase letters n and m

- Start at the red dot.
  Follow the arrows to write the letter.

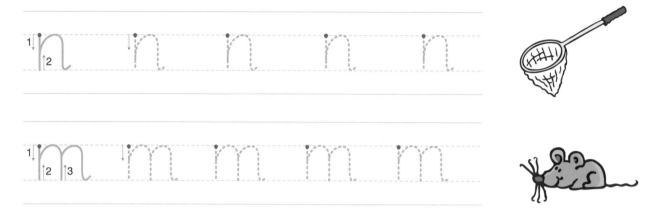

- With your pen take the monkey through the maze to reach the mangos.

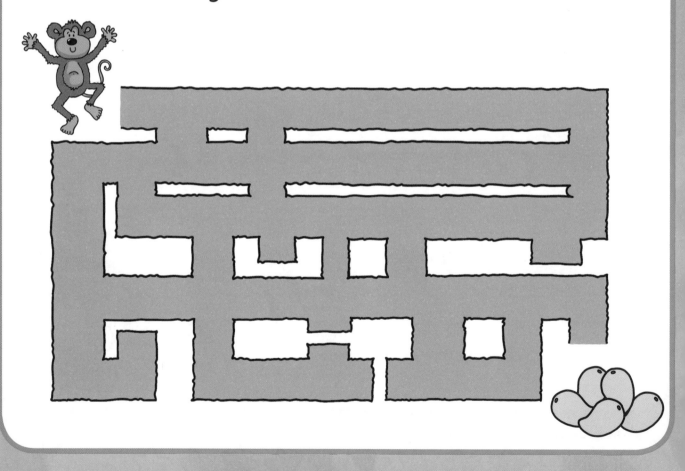

Using a sheet of sandpaper, cut out different letter shapes and stick each one to a square of card. Alternatively, you can make the letter shapes from pipe cleaners. Children love touching different textures. Encourage your child to use their finger to trace round the letter in the same way they would write it, forming the letter correctly.

Lowercase letters j and l

- Start at the red dot.
  Follow the arrows to write the letter.

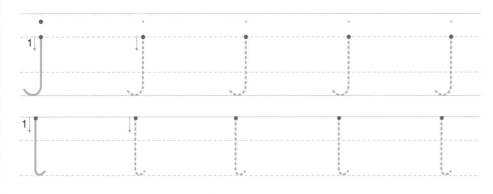

- Trace and colour the **jelly**, **jelly beans**, **jug**, **juice**, **jam**, **lion**, **leaves**, **ladybird**, **lemons** and **lolly**.

Well done!
Now colour
the star.

Lowercase letters t and h

- **Start at the red dot.**
  Follow the arrows to write the letter.

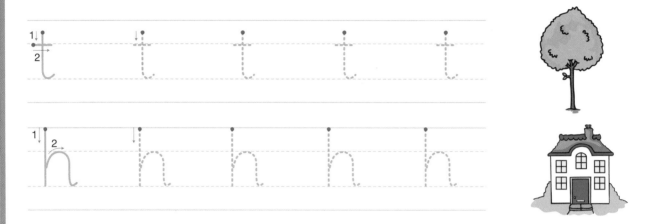

- **Trace the tent, hats and other triangles.**

Use a large cardboard box folded out flat for drawing on. Large-scale drawing is fun and encourages the use of the whole arm. Just drawing lines is fine. Your child doesn't have to draw anything recognisable – any mark making is good.

Lowercase letters k and f

- Start at the red dot.
  Follow the arrows to write the letter.

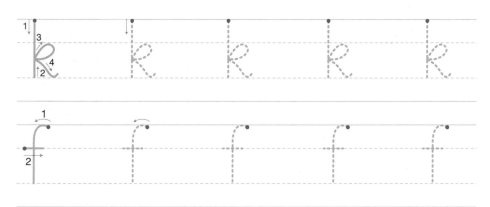

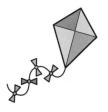

- Draw patterns on the **k**ites and **f**lags.

Well done!
Now colour
the star.

Lowercase letters b and s

● Start at the red dot.
  Follow the arrows to write the letter.

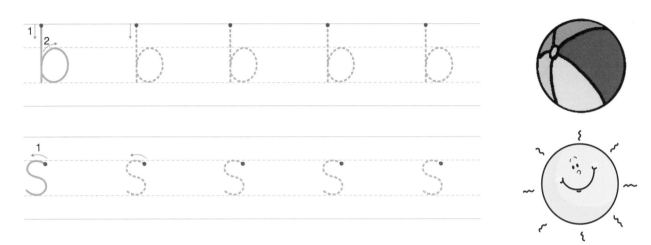

● Colour the pictures that start with **b** or **s**.

If you have a low, child-size table at home, try taping a large piece of paper to the underside of the table, so your child can lie on their back under the table and stretch up their arm to draw. This is a different, fun way of drawing and helps to develop lots of important muscles at the same time!

Lowercase letters e and q

- Start at the red dot.
  Follow the arrows to write the letter.

- Draw a crown for each **q**ueen and an **e**gg for each hen.

Well done!
Now colour
the star.

Lowercase letters p and y

● Start at the red dot.
  Follow the arrows to write the letter.

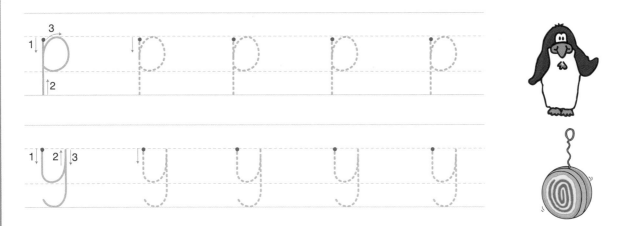

● Join the dots to draw a picture.

It is important for children to understand that writing has a purpose, especially in an electronic world where pens are often not needed! If you send cards to friends, let them add their own name too, even if it is not readable yet – it is still their mark and one we value.

Lowercase letters u, v and w

- Start at the red dot.
  Follow the arrows to write the letter.

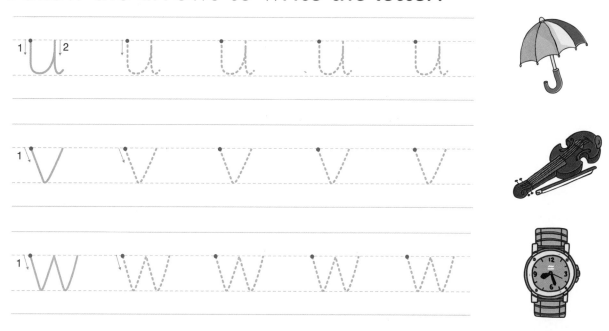

- Draw a line to match each letter to the correct picture.

u   v   w

Well done!
Now colour
the star.

Lowercase letters z and x

- Start at the red dot.
  Follow the arrows to write the letter.

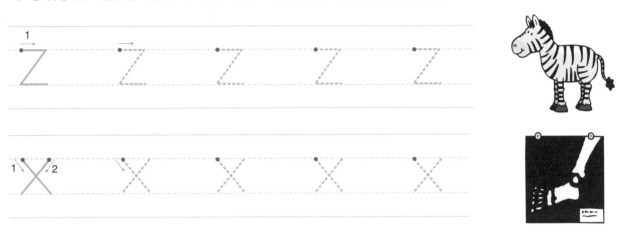

- Look at the picture of the zoo.
  Circle all the animals you see.
  Cross out (✗) all the things that should not be there.

On the next page, write your child's name on the top line for them to copy below. Even if they can already write their name, practising writing on lines and forming the letters correctly is very valuable. As an extension, you can write their surname or other familiar names.

Writing your name

- Practise writing your own name on the lines below. Make sure you form each letter correctly.

abcdefghijklmn

opqrstuvwxyz

My name is...

Well done! Now colour the star.

Writing capital letters A–M

● Trace and then copy each letter.
Start at the red dot.

Capital letters are easier to write than lowercase letters, but should be taught after lowercase. Children should learn that a capital is only used for the first letter of a name or at the start of a new sentence.

32

Writing capital letters N–Z

● Trace and then copy each letter.
Start at the red dot.

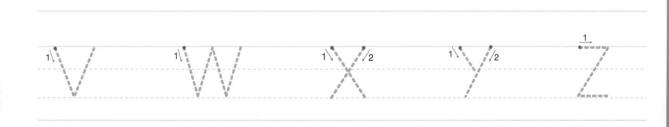

Well done!
Now colour
the star.

Missing letters

● Look at the alphabet.
Some letters are missing. Can you write them in?

a b __ d e __

g __ __ j k __

m n __ p q __

s __ u __ w x

y __

Your child is not expected to be able to read the words on the next page. They just need to know the starting letter, so they can complete each word. They are all phonetic starting sounds.

Which letter?

Write the missing letter to complete the word.

abcdefghijklmn
opqrstuvwxyz

 __pple

 __anana

 __rapes

 __range

 __ear

Well done!
Now colour
the star.

First words

● Write the correct word under each picture.
Choose from the words below.

cat   dog   bed

fox   bus   zip

— — — —   — — — —

— — — —   — — — —

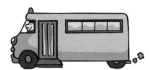   

— — — —   — — — —

If your child is new to phonics, help them sound out each letter to read the words and when they write them under each picture. If they still need help writing the letters, put the dots on the lines or write the letter in a yellow pen for them to trace over.

Writing numbers

- Start at the red dot.
  Follow the arrows to write the numbers.

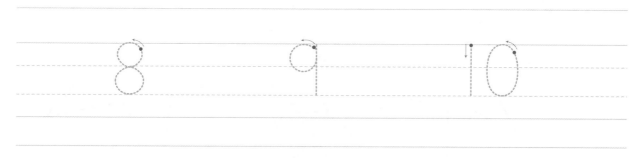

Well done!
Now colour
the star.

Colouring

- Colour the picture.

Felt-tip pens are often easier for children to use for colouring than crayons or pencils, as they do not have to press so hard to achieve a good result. If the tip is fine, they can do more intricate work and, therefore, find it easier to stay within the lines.

Dot-to-dot

- Start at number 1 and join the dots in order to finish the picture.
  Copy the picture in the box below.

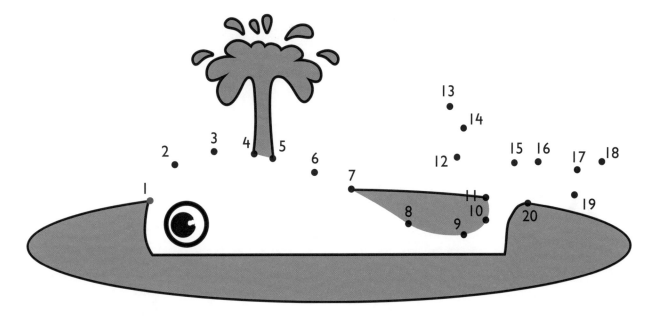

Well done!
Now colour
the star.

Matching letters A–M

- Write the matching lowercase letter next to each capital letter.

abcdefghijklmn
opqrstuvwxyz

A __   B __   C __

D __   E __   F __

G __   H __   I __

J __   K __   L __

M __

If your child needs to be reminded of the shape of the letter, use the alphabet at the top of the page. If they are still not sure, you can practise on a separate piece of paper or write it bigger for them to copy.

Matching letters N–Z

● Write the matching lowercase letter next to each capital letter.

abcdefghijklmn
opqrstuvwxyz

N __   O __   P __

Q __   R __   S __

T __   U __   V __

W __   X __   Y __

Z __

Well done!
Now colour
the star.

41

Cursive alphabet a–m

- Cursive writing is a different way of writing lowercase letters.
It helps to prepare you for joined-up writing.
Trace and copy the letters.

Most children will come across cursive writing early in their education. Some schools use it from the start, others teach it later on. It is good for your child to have seen the letters beforehand so, when it is introduced, it will not confuse and upset them. They will already know that the letters they are familiar with can be written in other ways. Capital letters are not included because they are never joined to the next letter.

Cursive alphabet n–z

- Trace and copy the letters.

Well done!
Now colour
the star.

Answers

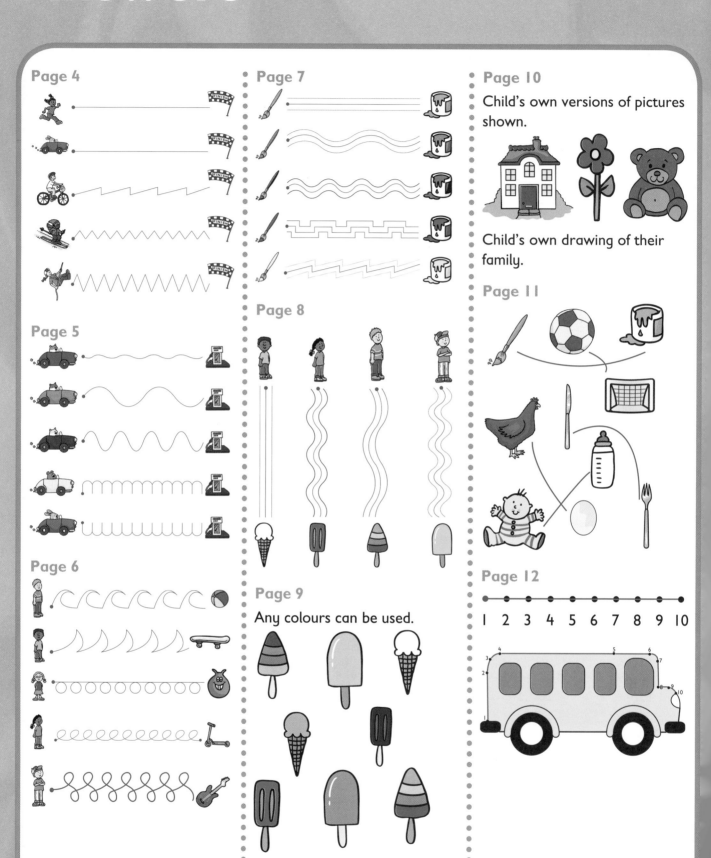

Page 4

Page 5

Page 6

Page 7

Page 8

Page 9

Any colours can be used.

Page 10

Child's own versions of pictures shown.

Child's own drawing of their family.

Page 11

Page 12

1 2 3 4 5 6 7 8 9 10

Answers

Page 13

Page 14

Child's own versions of shapes shown.

Page 15

Child's own versions of pictures shown.

Page 16–17

A ring drawn around the country where the child lives.

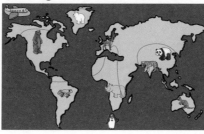

Page 18

Any colours can be used.

Page 19

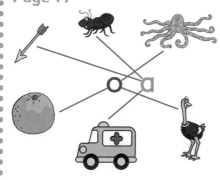
  o a

Page 20

duck   <u>d</u>og

goat   g<u>i</u>rl

Page 21

Page 22

Any alternative route can be taken.

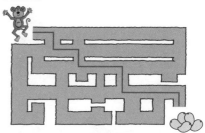

Page 23

Page 24

Answers

Page 25
Child's own patterns drawn on the flags and kites.

Page 26
Any colours can be used.

Page 27

Page 28
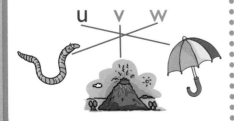

Page 29
u v w

Page 30

Page 31
Child's own name.

Page 32–33
All capital letters traced and copied.

Page 34
a b <u>c</u> <u>d</u> e <u>f</u>
g <u>h</u> <u>i</u> j k <u>l</u>
m n <u>o</u> p q <u>r</u>
s <u>t</u> u <u>v</u> w x
y <u>z</u>

Page 35
 <u>a</u>pple

 <u>b</u>anana

 <u>g</u>rapes

 <u>o</u>range

 <u>p</u>ear

Page 36

<u>c</u> <u>a</u> <u>t</u>   <u>b</u> <u>e</u> <u>d</u>

<u>z</u> <u>i</u> <u>p</u>   <u>d</u> <u>o</u> <u>g</u>

<u>b</u> <u>u</u> <u>s</u>   <u>f</u> <u>o</u> <u>x</u>

Page 37
All numbers traced and copied.

Answers

Page 38

Any colours can be used.

Page 39

Child's own version of picture.

Page 40

A <u>a</u> B <u>b</u> C <u>c</u>

D <u>d</u> E <u>e</u> F <u>f</u>

G <u>g</u> H <u>h</u> I <u>i</u>

J <u>j</u> K <u>k</u> L <u>l</u>

M <u>m</u>

Page 41

N <u>n</u> O <u>o</u> P <u>p</u>

Q <u>q</u> R <u>r</u> S <u>s</u>

T <u>t</u> U <u>u</u> V <u>v</u>

W <u>w</u> X <u>x</u> Y <u>y</u>

Z <u>z</u>

Page 42–43

All cursive letters traced and copied.

Collins Easy Learning

Certificate of Achievement

Well Done!

This certificate is awarded to ....

for successfully completing ....

Age ....

Date ....

Signed ....

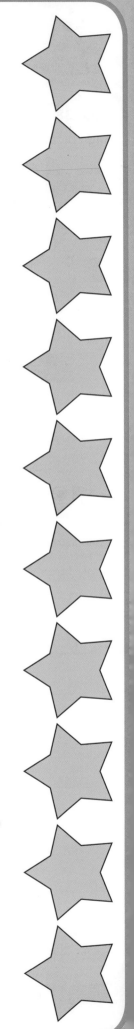